DESSERTS

DESSERTS

50 Recipes from the
Chicago Tribune

TRIBUNE
PUBLISHING
ORLANDO / 1993

CHICAGO TRIBUNE
Carol Haddix: Food Guide Editor
JeanMarie Brownson:
Associate Food Guide Editor

Cover photograph by Bill Hogan
Back cover photograph by Tony Berardi

Inside photographs by
Tony Berardi, Bob Fila,
Bill Hogan, Chris Walker

Cover design by Bill Henderson,
Tribune Publishing

Copyright © 1993
Tribune Publishing
75 East Amelia Street
Orlando, Florida 32801

Printed in Mexico by
R.R. Donnelley & Sons, Inc.

FIRST EDITION

Library of Congress
Cataloging-in-Publication Data
Desserts : 50 recipes from the Chicago tribune.
    p.   cm.
  Includes index.
  ISBN 0-941263-62-2 : $18.95
  1. Desserts.   2. Chicago tribune
TX773.D4775 1993
641.8'6--dc20   92-40233
                 CIP

TRIBUNE PUBLISHING
Editorial Director: George C. Biggers III
Managing Editor: Dixie Kasper
Senior Editor: Kathleen M. Kiely
Production Editor: Ken Paskman
Designer: Bill Henderson

For information:
Tribune Publishing
P.O. Box 1100
Orlando, Florida 32801

Creating a newspaper food section and assorted food columns every week takes teamwork. The following people have contributed their enthusiasm and skills to the task, making this book the work of many:

Thanks to
Jack Fuller, Howard Tyner and Brenda Butler for leadership;
Steven Pratt and Connie Coning for editing prowess;
William Rice, Pat Dailey and Barbara Sullivan
for lively reporting and writing;
Patti Florez for food styling with flair;
Bob Fila, Bill Hogan and Tony Berardi
for capturing the flavor of food on film;
Kevin Fewell for creative art direction;
Richard Rott, Karen Blair and Mary Wilson for research work
and Terry Smith for her willing secretarial support.

– Carol Haddix
JeanMarie Brownson

CONTENTS

America loves desserts. And despite the talk about dieting and eating right, dessert is one popular way to treat ourselves. What party would be complete without something sweet?

When it comes to entertaining, the grand finale is as important as the first exquisite appetizer. With dessert comes the added opportunity to dazzle, to leave guests with a lasting impression.

No wonder so many cooks spend so much time looking for just the right dessert recipe. The majority of calls and letters to the *Chicago Tribune* test kitchen are requests for wonderful, foolproof desserts.

A reader forgot to clip that wonderful ice cream recipe, perhaps, or someone in the family threw out the recipe for a chocolate mousse cake that would be perfect for Aunt Sue's visit.

This collection of recipes we've gathered from recent pages of the *Chicago Tribune* includes a nod or two toward the new concerns about eating light. A tart lemon-lime mousse and a flavorful low-fat pound cake are just two recipes that no one need feel guilty about eating.

But most of these tested recipes are for those times when the cook wants to splurge on friends and family. A sinfully rich cashew and hazelnut tart or a decadently silky white-chocolate cheesecake are the perfect answers.

The recipes are divided by chapters into the flavors we so often crave: chocolate, vanilla, nuts and fruits, and the basics that form the foundation of so many classic desserts. Now, let the entertaining begin.

CHOCOLATE

This easy dessert from columnist Abby Mandel is satisfying but not as rich as many other chocolate desserts. The thinnest sheets of chocolate are used in the same way as puff pastry is used in the classic mille-feuille recipe; they can be cut into rectangles to resemble Napoleons or into any other shape.

Preparation time: 25 minutes
Chilling time: 30 minutes
Yield: 4 servings

---

4 ounces bittersweet or semisweet chocolate

2 teaspoons safflower oil

1 package (10 ounces) frozen raspberries, thawed, pureed, strained, chilled

1 teaspoon raspberry liqueur, optional

1 pint raspberry sorbet, ice cream or frozen yogurt

$1/2$ pint raspberries

1 teaspoon confectioners' sugar

1. Grease cookie sheet and line with parchment paper. It's important that the paper stay flat; weight it at the corners, if necessary. Use a pencil to trace a 9-by-7-inch rectangle on the paper. Set aside.

2. Melt chocolate and oil in top of double boiler set over gently simmering water or in a microwave oven in microwave-safe dish on medium-high (75 percent) power. Stir just until smooth. Pour into center of rectangle. Quickly spread chocolate with small rubber spatula to fill rectangle. Refrigerate until firm, about 30 minutes.

3. Use pizza cutter to cut lengthwise in half. Then cut crosswise into 4 equal pieces. You will have 8 rectangles, about $3 1/2$ inches by $2 1/4$ inches. Or cut chocolate into any other desired shapes. Carefully peel pieces off paper and transfer to airtight tin, placing piece of wax paper in between. Refrigerate or freeze. Use thawed but chilled.

4. To assemble, combine pureed raspberries with liqueur. Swirl enough raspberry sauce on dessert plate to coat. Let sorbet, ice cream or frozen yogurt soften just enough so it's scoopable but not runny. Place piece of chocolate in center of plate. Arrange scoop(s) as desired. Top loosely with another chocolate piece, perhaps at an angle. Sieve a thin coating of confectioners' sugar on top of chocolate. Arrange raspberries on sauce. Serve immediately. Offer any remaining sauce on the side.

This knockout dessert (chocolate custard layered with chocolate hearts) is from Mary Beth Liccioni, pastry chef and co-owner of Le Francais restaurant, Wheeling, Illinois. It is perfect for a special Valentine's Day dinner. Yes, the gold is edible. The chocolate hearts can be made ahead and stored in a cool, dry place.

Preparation time: 1 hour
Chilling time: Overnight
Cooking time: 65 minutes
Yield: 4 servings

CHOCOLATE HEARTS

6 ounces bittersweet or semisweet chocolate, melted, cooled to lukewarm

CHOCOLATE CUSTARD

2 cups half-and-half

1/2 cup sugar

6 large egg yolks

1 large whole egg

4 ounces bittersweet chocolate, melted

Edible gold leaf (see note) or unsweetened cocoa powder

1. For the hearts, cover a large cookie sheet (or the bottom of a jelly-roll pan) with plastic wrap, taking care so the plastic is tight and smooth. Secure by taping it on the underside of the baking sheet. Pour enough chocolate to make a very thin, even layer, spreading it with the edge of a large metal spatula. Allow to harden for several hours.

2. Carefully cut 12 or more hearts from the chocolate, using a sharp metal cookie cutter. It probably will be necessary to run a small, sharp knife around the cutter so you get a smooth, clean cut. You will need three hearts for each serving. There may be extra hearts. Set the hearts aside in a cool place.

3. For the custard, heat oven to 300 degrees. Heat half-and-half with sugar in saucepan until hot but not boiling. Whisk egg yolks and egg in a medium bowl. Whisking as you do so, add the hot half-and-half mixture to eggs, then add the melted chocolate. Pour through a fine wire mesh strainer into a 1-quart glass baking dish; skim foam.

4. Place baking dish in a larger, shallow baking pan; add hot water to the larger pan so it comes halfway up sides of baking dish. Bake until custard is just barely set in the center, about 65 minutes. Remove from water and cool on wire rack. Cover and refrigerate overnight.

5. To serve, place a heart on a serving plate and smooth a layer of chocolate custard over. Center with a heart, another layer of custard and finally, a chocolate heart. (If any hearts break, they can be used as the center layer.) Lightly brush top heart with gold leaf or sift cocoa powder over top.

Note: Edible gold leaf can be ordered from Wehrung & Billmeier, 1924 Eddy St. Chicago, IL 60657. Call 312-472-1544.

This is chocolate artist and teacher Elaine Gonzalez's special version of a light yet fancy company dessert that is sure to please guests.

Preparation time: 30 minutes
Chilling time: Several hours
Yield: 8 servings

---

3 cups whipping cream

3 tablespoons granulated sugar

2 teaspoons instant espresso coffee granules

4 large eggs

2 tablespoons brandy

1 package (12 ounces) semisweet chocolate chips

1/2 cup confectioners' sugar

Ground cinnamon

Chocolate sauce, see page 98, optional

Strawberry sauce, see page 98, optional

1. Heat 1 cup of the cream, granulated sugar and espresso granules in a heavy saucepan until simmering and sugar is dissolved. Whisk eggs in a small bowl; whisk some of the hot cream mixture into the eggs to warm them. Then whisk egg mixture back into remaining cream. Cook and stir over low heat just until mixture thickens enough to lightly coat the back of a spoon. Do not boil. Remove from heat; stir in brandy. Stir in chocolate chips until melted.

2. Pour into bowl, cool and cover. Chill in refrigerator for several hours or overnight.

3. Before serving, beat the remaining 2 cups of whipping cream until soft peaks form when beaters are lifted; add confectioners' sugar and continue beating until cream is thick.

4. Gently fold 1/2 of the whipped cream into the chocolate mixture to lighten it. Spoon mousse into chocolate cups or onto serving dishes. Top with remaining whipped cream and sprinkle with cinnamon. Spoon chocolate and/or strawberry sauce around mousse, if desired.

This moist, fudgelike cake may be baked ahead. You also can vary the flavor by changing the liqueur. Orange liqueur, white or dark rum (add a tablespoon of instant espresso powder with dark rum), or 2 teaspoons of vanilla extract instead of the alcohol will all work well. The recipe is from pastry chef Nick Malgieri, an instructor at Peter Kump's Cooking School in New York City.

Preparation time: 30 minutes
Cooking time: 45 to 55 minutes
Chilling time: Several hours or overnight
Yield: 10 servings

---

12 ounces bittersweet or semisweet chocolate

1/2 cup sugar

1/3 cup water

1 cup (2 sticks) unsalted butter, softened

4 large eggs, lightly beaten

1/4 cup framboise (raspberry eau de vie) or desired liqueur

GARNISH

1 cup whipping cream

2 tablespoons sugar

1/2 pint fresh raspberries, optional

Mint sprigs

1. Heat oven to 300 degrees. Butter an 8-inch round pan, at least 2 inches deep, and line the bottom with parchment or wax paper cut to fit. Butter the paper. Chop chocolate very finely and set it aside.

2. Put sugar and water into a saucepan; heat to boil over low heat, stirring occasionally so all the sugar crystals dissolve. Remove from heat; stir in butter and chocolate. Cover pan and allow to stand 5 minutes. Whisk until smooth.

3. Whisk eggs and liqueur into chocolate mixture in a stream, being careful not to overmix.

4. Pour batter into prepared pan. Place the pan in a larger baking pan containing 1 inch of warm water. Bake until set and slightly dry on the surface, 45 to 55 minutes. (A wooden pick will not come out clean.) Cool to room temperature in the pan and cover with plastic wrap. Refrigerate in pan until cold or up to several days (or freeze up to 1 month). Let stand 1 hour at room temperature before serving.

5. To unmold, run a knife between the dessert and the pan and immerse the bottom of the pan in hot water. Invert onto a platter.

6. To garnish, beat cream and sugar until soft peaks form. Spread over cake and arrange berries and mint leaves around edge.

*Students at La Varenne Cooking School at Chateau du Fey in Burgundy often
learn to prepare this elegant chocolate cake roll.*

Preparation time: 45 minutes
Cooking time: 10 minutes
Chilling time: Several hours
Yield: 8 to 10 servings

---

5 tablespoons all-purpose flour

1/4 cup unsweetened cocoa powder

1/2 teaspoon salt

3 large eggs, plus 3 egg yolks

1/2 cup granulated sugar

1/2 teaspoon vanilla extract

1 pound semisweet chocolate

1 1/3 cups whipping cream

Confectioners' sugar for garnish

1. Heat the oven to 375 degrees. Grease a 15-by-10-inch baking sheet, line it with wax paper and grease the paper. Sift flour and cocoa with salt.

2. Put eggs and egg yolks in a large bowl and whisk until mixed. Add sugar and beat with an electric mixer, until mixture is light and thick enough to leave a ribbon trail when the beater is lifted, 8 to 10 minutes. Add vanilla and stir to combine. Sift flour mixture over the batter, a third at a time, folding in each addition with a rubber spatula as lightly as possible.

3. Spread batter evenly over prepared pan. Bake until edges are browned, 8 to 10 minutes. (Do not overbake or cake will crack when rolled.)

4. While still hot, gently invert cake onto a clean dish towel. Remove paper and roll up the long side of the warm cake with the towel. Leave it rolled up to cool.

5. Chop chocolate into pieces and place in a heat-resistant bowl. Heat cream just to a boil, then pour over broken chocolate. Stir gently until chocolate has melted. Let cool, then beat with an electric mixer until filling is light and very smooth, about 5 minutes.

6. Unroll cooled cake and trim edges. Spread a layer of chocolate filling on the cake and roll it back up evenly. Transfer to a platter, seam side down. Coat roll with remaining filling, smoothing it until even. Trim ends of roll and refrigerate until cold. When firm, cover loosely with plastic wrap. This roll can be made up to 48 hours ahead and refrigerated.

7. Just before serving, sprinkle roll lightly with confectioners' sugar.

Although white chocolate is not really chocolate, you'd have a hard time trying to convince fans of the sweet confection that it's only a pale imitation of the real thing. The following rich cheesecake will only cement their devotion.

Preparation time: 1 hour
Cooking time: 1 hour and
35 minutes
Yield: 12 servings

---

4 packages (8 ounces each) cream cheese, softened

1 cup sugar

$1/2$ cup sour cream

6 large eggs

$1/3$ cup whipping cream

8 ounces white chocolate, partly melted so small chunks still remain

1 tablespoon vanilla extract

GARNISH

8 ounces white chocolate (see note)

1. Heat oven to 250 degrees. Wrap the exterior of a 10-inch springform pan with a double thickness of heavy-duty aluminum foil. (This is to prevent water from seeping into pan when it gets baked in a pan of water.) Generously butter the interior of the pan.

2. Beat cream cheese in large bowl of electric mixer until soft and light. Add sugar and continue beating until smooth. Add sour cream and mix again until smooth. Beat in eggs, 2 at a time, beating well after each addition. Pour in whipping cream and mix well. Beat in partly melted white chocolate; add vanilla and mix well.

3. Spoon batter into prepared springform pan. Put the springform pan into a slightly larger baking pan. Pour enough water into the baking pan to come $1/8$-inch of the way up the springform pan.

4. Bake until set but cake still wiggles slightly in center, about 1 hour and 35 minutes. Remove from oven and allow cheesecake to cool for 30 minutes at room temperature. Refrigerate until cold, several hours or overnight.

5. Make chocolate curls and shavings by drawing vegetable peeler over an 8-ounce bar of white chocolate. Use this to decorate top of cheesecake.

Note: If white chocolate is not the desired garnish, beat 1 cup whipping cream with a little confectioners' sugar until stiff. Use to frost cheesecake.

This sundae makes a perfect summer dessert. It's a take-off on the famous Italian dessert so popular in restaurants now, but we think it's better.

Preparation time: 25 minutes
Freezing time: Up to 1 hour
Yield: 4 servings

1$^1\!/_2$ cups whipping cream

2 tablespoons confectioners' sugar

6 ounces mascarpone cheese or 2 packages (3 ounces each) cream cheese, softened

1$^1\!/_2$ to 1$^2\!/_3$ cups crumbled lady-fingers (see note)

$^1\!/_4$ cup cold, extra-strong brewed coffee or espresso

2 to 4 tablespoons dark rum to taste

8 scoops premium coffee ice cream

$^1\!/_4$ cup shaved bittersweet (not unsweetened) chocolate

Chocolate sauce, see page 98 or bottled

Chocolate curls for garnish

1. Beat cream in large bowl of electric mixer until frothy. Beat in confectioners' sugar until soft peaks form. Transfer whipped cream to a large wire mesh strainer lined with a coffee filter or cheesecloth; set strainer over a bowl. Refrigerate up to several hours.

2. Put cheese into small bowl of electric mixer; beat until light and fluffy. Beat in about $^1\!/_2$ of the whipped cream until smooth and light.

3. To assemble, divide crumbled ladyfingers among 4 serving dishes. Sprinkle each with 1 tablespoon of the coffee and $^1\!/_2$ to 1 tablespoon of the dark rum. Top each with $^1\!/_4$ of the cheese mixture and 2 scoops of the ice cream. Freeze up to 1 hour before serving.

4. To serve, spoon some chocolate sauce over each serving. Dollop or pipe some whipped cream over each; sprinkle with 1 tablespoon of the shaved chocolate. Garnish with chocolate curl and serve immediately.

Note: Ladyfingers for tiramisu, such as savoiardi made by Bistefani in Italy, are available at Italian specialty markets and some supermarkets. Other ladyfingers or crumbled pound cake can be substituted.

Souffles need not be a cause for concern for home cooks. The following recipe is very easy to follow, satisfying and – as you will soon discover – remarkably good.

Preparation time: 25 minutes
Cooking time: 10 to 12 minutes
Yield: 4 to 6 servings

---

4 ounces semisweet chocolate

¼ cup (½ stick) unsalted butter

4 large eggs, separated

Granulated sugar

Confectioners' sugar

1. Place chocolate and butter in a saucepan and allow to melt over low heat.

2. Remove pan from heat and stir in egg yolks until chocolate thickens slightly. Pour into large mixing bowl.

3. Beat egg whites until stiff. Fold half of the whites into the chocolate mixture. Add remaining whites and fold in.

4. Butter the inside of a low-sided, 1-quart souffle mold and coat the surface lightly with granulated sugar. Pour in the mousse mixture. Recipe may be done ahead to this point. Store in the refrigerator until ready to bake.

5. Heat oven to 475 degrees. Place souffle in oven and bake for 5 minutes. Reduce heat to 425 degrees and continue baking 5 to 7 minutes more. Sprinkle with confectioners' sugar and serve at once.

VANILLA

Jeanne Jones is a nationally syndicated writer whose mission is to make healthful dishes out of recipes that are high in fat, sodium and cholesterol. This recipe is her very successful version of vanilla poundcake. One slice contains 169 calories, negligible cholesterol, 6 grams fat, and 181 milligrams sodium.

Preparation time: 20 minutes
Cooking time: 1 hour
Yield: 16 $^1/_2$-inch slices

2$^1/_4$ cups unbleached all-purpose flour

$^3/_4$ teaspoon baking powder

$^1/_4$ teaspoon each: baking soda, salt

$^1/_8$ teaspoon ground mace, optional

$^1/_2$ cup (1 stick) corn-oil margarine, softened

1 cup sugar

3 egg whites

1$^1/_2$ teaspoons vanilla extract

$^3/_4$ cup buttermilk

1. Heat oven to 350 degrees. Put flour, baking powder, baking soda, salt and mace into medium bowl. Mix well and set aside.

2. Cream margarine and sugar in large mixer bowl until smooth. Beat in egg whites and vanilla until satin smooth. Alternately add flour mixture and buttermilk in two additions each, blending well after each addition.

3. Spoon batter into an 8-by-4$^1/_2$-inch loaf pan sprayed with non-stick vegetable spray. Bake until cake is golden and has pulled away from sides of pan, about 1 hour. Cool on wire rack.

When fresh summer fruits come into season, this dessert is ideal for showcasing them. Take your pick from fresh, ripe strawberries, peaches or any of your favorites. If time is a problem, canned or frozen fruit can be substituted.

Preparation time: 40 minutes
Cooking time: 12 to 15 minutes
Yield: 10 to 12 servings

VANILLA CAKE

1 cup sifted cake flour

1 teaspoon baking powder

¼ teaspoon salt

3 large eggs

1 cup granulated sugar

⅓ cup water

2 teaspoons vanilla extract

FRUIT FILLING

1 package (8 ounces) cream cheese, softened

½ cup confectioners' sugar, sifted

1 teaspoon vanilla extract

1 vanilla bean

1 cup finely diced, peeled fresh fruit, such as peaches, nectarines, kiwi or hulled strawberries

Vanilla sugar for garnish, see page 99

1. Heat oven to 375 degrees. Line a 15-by-10-inch jellyroll pan with greased wax paper. For cake, sift together cake flour, baking powder and salt in small bowl; set aside.

2. Beat eggs in large bowl of electric mixer on high speed until thick and lemon-colored, about 5 minutes. Gradually beat in granulated sugar. Add water and vanilla and beat on low speed. Gradually add dry ingredients, beating just until batter is smooth.

3. Spread batter evenly in prepared pan. Bake until top springs back when touched lightly, 12 to 15 minutes.

4. Remove cake from oven and loosen cake from edges of pan. Immediately invert cake onto a clean towel that has been sprinkled heavily with confectioners' sugar. Carefully remove wax paper. Trim off stiff edges of cake if neccessary. While cake is hot, use the towel to roll it, beginning with the narrow end. Let cake cool completely wrapped in the towel on wire rack.

5. For fruit filling, beat cream cheese in small bowl of electric mixer until smooth and fluffy. Add sifted confectioners' sugar and mix well. Add vanilla and mix well. Cut vanilla bean lengthwise in half; use the tip of a paring knife to scrape out the seeds into the cheese mixture (reserve the bean for making vanilla sugar). Beat to blend. Gently fold in prepared fruit.

6. When cake has cooled, carefully unroll cake and spread with fruit mixture. Carefully roll cake up again. Generously sprinkle with vanilla sugar. Wrap loosely with towel and store in refrigerator until serving time or up to several hours.

PUMPKIN TORTE WITH VANILLA CREAM

Chelsea Williams, a talented home cook from Missouri, created a new way to use pumpkin in this delectable torte. This adaptation of her recipe uses vanilla wafers in the crust and a creamy vanilla filling.

Preparation time: 1 hour
Cooking time: 20 minutes
Chilling time: 2 hours or overnight
Yield: 8 to 10 servings

CRUST

$^1/_2$ cup melted butter

$1^3/_4$ cups crushed vanilla wafers

$^1/_3$ cup granulated sugar

CREAM LAYER

2 large eggs, beaten

$^3/_4$ cup granulated sugar

1 package (8 ounces) cream cheese, softened

2 teaspoons vanilla extract

PUMPKIN FILLING

1 can (16 ounces) solid-packed pumpkin

3 large eggs, separated, at room temperature

$^3/_4$ cup granulated sugar

$^1/_2$ cup milk

$^1/_2$ teaspoon salt

1 teaspoon cinnamon

1 envelope gelatin, dissolved in $^1/_4$ cup cold water

GARNISH

1 cup whipping cream

1 tablespoon confectioners' sugar

2 teaspoons vanilla extract

1. Heat oven to 350 degrees. For the crust, mix the melted butter, crushed cookies and $^1/_3$ cup sugar in small bowl. Press mixture over bottom and halfway up sides of a 9-inch springform pan.

2. For cream layer, beat eggs, $^3/_4$ cup sugar, cream cheese and vanilla in medium bowl with electric mixer until smooth. Pour over the crust. Bake in the center of the oven until firm, 18 to 20 minutes. Cool on wire rack.

3. For pumpkin filling, put pumpkin, egg yolks, $^1/_2$ cup of the sugar, milk, salt and cinnamon in medium saucepan. Blend together and cook over medium heat, stirring often, until bubbling. Off the heat, stir in the dissolved gelatin. Set aside to cool to room temperature.

4. Beat the egg whites until frothy. Gradually beat in remaining $^1/_4$ cup sugar until stiff – but not dry – peaks form.

5. Fold egg whites into the pumpkin mixture. Pour the mixture over the baked crust and cream layer. Refrigerate until set, at least 2 hours or overnight.

6. Up to 1 hour before serving, beat cream in large bowl of electric mixer until frothy; beat in confectioners' sugar and vanilla until soft peaks form. Remove sides of springform pan. Spread some of the cream over top of cake. Use a pastry bag to pipe out remaining cream in a decorative border. Serve cold.

Rich vanilla pudding, layered with fresh raspberries and crisp cookies, makes this colorful parfait elegant enough for a dinner party.

Preparation time: 30 minutes
Cooking time: 15 minutes
Chilling time: Several hours
Yield: 6 to 8 servings

VANILLA CREAM FILLING

1 cup granulated sugar

$1/2$ cup all-purpose flour

$1/4$ teaspoon salt

3 cups milk

4 large egg yolks

3 tablespoons unsalted butter

$1^1/2$ teaspoons vanilla extract

RASPBERRY FILLING

4 cups fresh raspberries

1 cup granulated sugar

2 tablespoons cornstarch

COOKIE CRUMBS

$1^1/2$ cups crushed vanilla cookies or shortbread cookies

$1/2$ cup finely chopped pecans

1 cup whipped cream for garnish

1. For vanilla cream filling, put sugar, flour and salt in a saucepan. Gradually stir in milk. Cook over medium heat, whisking constantly, until mixture simmers and thickens. Reduce heat to low and cook a minute longer. Beat egg yolks in a bowl and stir in some of the hot milk mixture. Add contents of bowl to pan with remaining milk mixture. Cook and stir until simmering. Remove pan from heat and stir in butter and vanilla. Transfer to a bowl to cool, covering the top with plastic wrap to prevent a skin from forming. Refrigerate until cold or up to several days.

2. For raspberry filling, put raspberries, sugar and cornstarch in a medium non-aluminum saucepan. Cook and stir over medium heat until mixture simmers and thickens. Transfer to a bowl; cool to room temperature.

3. For cookie crumbs, mix crushed cookies with chopped pecans.

4. To assemble the parfaits, spoon about $1/4$ cup raspberry filling into the bottom of 6 or 8 parfait or wine glasses. Sprinkle about 2 tablespoons of crumb mixture onto the filling in each glass. Add about $1/4$ cup cream filling to each glass. Repeat with remaining fillings and crumbs, dividing each equally among the glasses.

5. Chill desserts until ready to serve. Just before serving, decorate the top of each parfait with whipped cream.

Despite the hundreds of different flavored cheesecakes you can find today, there is something comforting about the classic cheesecake, made with pure vanilla and topped with strawberries. Also try it with fresh blueberries or sliced peaches.

Preparation time: 30 minutes
Baking time: 1½ hours
Cooling time: 1 hour
Chilling time: 4 hours or more
Yield: 16 servings

¼ cup vanilla wafer cookie crumbs

1¼ cups plus 2 tablespoons granulated sugar

½ teaspoon cinnamon

2 packages (8 ounces each) cream cheese, softened

½ cup all-purpose flour

6 large eggs, separated

1 cup sour cream

2 teaspoons vanilla extract

Seeds from 1 vanilla bean, optional

½ teaspoon cream of tartar

Pinch salt

Confectioners' sugar

Fresh strawberries for garnish

1. Heat oven to 325 degrees. Generously butter bottom of 10-inch springform pan. Mix cookie crumbs, 2 tablespoons of the sugar and cinnamon in small bowl. Sprinkle over bottom of prepared pan.

2. Beat cream cheese in large bowl of electric mixer until light and fluffy. Beat in ¾ cup of the sugar and the flour. Beat in egg yolks. Beat in sour cream, vanilla extract and vanilla seeds.

3. Beat egg whites, cream of tartar and salt in large mixer bowl until foamy. Gradually beat in remaining ½ cup sugar until stiff peaks form. Fold into cheese mixture. Turn into prepared pan.

4. Put springform pan on rack set in larger pan. Add water to larger pan to rack level but not touching springform pan. Bake until center of cake is set but still wiggles, about 1½ hours. Turn off oven; let cool with door slightly ajar for 1 hour. Remove. Cool to room temperature.

5. Refrigerate until cold, at least 4 hours. To serve, loosen cake from sides of pan with a spatula. Remove sides of pan. Sprinkle generously with confectioners' sugar. Garnish with strawberries.

Judy Contino, owner of Bittersweet Bakery in Chicago, makes these individual tarts for special occasions. She uses pate sucree, a rich, fragile French pastry. You can make a pate sucree using any recipe, or opt for our shortcut that uses crushed cookie crumbs instead. To make the free-form chocolate lattice garnish, drizzle melted bittersweet chocolate from the tines of a fork over a wax paper-lined baking sheet. Let stand until set and then carefully peel away paper. Store in a tin or box until needed.

Preparation time: 45 minutes
Cooking time: 20 minutes
Chilling time: Overnight
Yield: 4 servings

PASTRY SHELLS

1 recipe pate sucree;
or
3 ounces crisp vanilla cookies
3 tablespoons melted butter

CREME BRULEE CUSTARD

2 large egg yolks
2 tablespoons sugar
1/2 cup whipping cream
1/4 cup creme fraiche, see page 99
1/4 of a vanilla bean, split open
2 tablespoons unsalted butter, softened, cut in 3 pieces

ASSEMBLY

2 ounces bittersweet (not unsweetened) chocolate, melted
1 cup raspberries
Mint leaves

1. Roll out pastry and fit into four 3-inch tart pans. Line with parchment paper and fill with dried beans; bake as directed in pastry recipe. Or, if using cookies, crush cookies to a fine powder in a food processor or blender. Add butter to cookie crumbs and mix well. Press mixture into bottom and sides of four 3-inch tart pans. Bake in a 350-degree oven until set, about 8 minutes. Cool before using.

2. For creme brulee custard, whisk together the egg yolks, sugar, cream and creme fraiche in the top of a double boiler; add vanilla bean. Cook over gently simmering water until mixture is thick enough to coat a wooden spoon. Remove from heat and whisk in butter, one piece at a time. Strain into a bowl and chill overnight.

3. To assemble the tarts, brush the inside of the pastry shells with a thin layer of melted chocolate. For each tart, cut 3 raspberries in half and place the halves in the pastry.

4. Using a pastry bag with a round tip or a spoon, fill the pastry shells with the chilled creme brulee custard. Place a small cluster of berries in the center and add a sprig of mint. Add tiny chocolate hearts if desired.

Not many baked desserts work well in a microwave oven. But this light version of the French dessert, oeufs a la neige or "eggs in the snow," works wonderfully. It is from chef Jean Joho of the Everest Room in Chicago.

Preparation time: 25 minutes
Cooking time: 20 minutes
Chilling time: Several hours
Yield: 4 servings

CREME ANGLAISE SAUCE

$2^1/4$ cups milk

6 large egg yolks

6 tablespoons sugar

$1/2$ vanilla bean, split

SNOW EGGS

1 cup egg whites, about 5 large

$1/2$ cup sugar

CARAMEL GARNISH

1 cup sugar

1. For creme anglaise sauce, put milk into large microwave-safe bowl. Microwave on high (100 percent) power until simmering, about 4 minutes. (Or, heat milk in a heavy-bottomed saucepan.)

2. Beat egg yolks and 6 tablespoons sugar in small bowl of electric mixer until mixture is thick and light and falls in ribbons from the beaters, 5 to 10 minutes. Very slowly beat in the hot milk; add the vanilla bean.

3. Microwave, uncovered, on medium (50 percent) power, stirring vigorously every 2 minutes, until sauce is smooth and thickened just enough to lightly coat the back of a spoon, 8 to 10 minutes. (Or, cook mixture in the saucepan over low heat, stirring constantly.) It is very important to stir the sauce to prevent curdling. Immediately strain sauce through a fine wire mesh strainer into a bowl. Cover with plastic wrap touching the surface and refrigerate until thoroughly chilled.

4. For snow eggs, beat egg whites and $1/2$ cup sugar in large bowl of electric mixer until stiff but not dry. Use two large spoons dipped in warm water to shape mixture into large ovals (you will need 12 ovals). Carefully put 2 ovals onto a microwave-safe plate. Microwave on high until set, about 15 seconds. (Or, poach snow eggs in barely simmering water in a large saucepan over medium-low heat, turning over once, just until set, 1 to 2 minutes. Remove from the water with a slotted spatula and drain on a wax paper-lined baking sheet.)

5. Repeat to shape and cook remaining egg white mixture. (Snow eggs can be made up to 3 hours in advance of serving; let stand uncovered on a plate in a cool place. Do not refrigerate.)

6. To serve, pour about $1/2$ cup of the creme anglaise sauce onto a large serving plate or bowl. Top with 3 of the snow eggs. Repeat to fill all 4 serving plates.

7. For caramel, put sugar into a medium saucepan. Cook, stirring constantly, over medium-high heat until sugar melts completely and turns a light caramel color. Using a fork, immediately drizzle the hot caramelized sugar in a random pattern over the snow eggs. Serve as soon as caramel cools.

This simple poundcake, topped with a fresh berry sauce and garnished with more berries, is from Judy Contino, owner of Bittersweet Bakery in Chicago.

Preparation time: 45 minutes
Cooking time: 50 to 60 minutes
Yield: 6 to 8 servings

FRESH BERRY SAUCE

1 pint each: raspberries, hulled strawberries

$1/3$ cup sugar, or to taste

1 to 2 pinches ground cinnamon

1 teaspoon vanilla extract

POUNDCAKE

$3/4$ cup ($1^1/2$ sticks) plus 1 tablespoon unsalted butter, softened

$2/3$ cup sugar

3 large eggs

$1/2$ cup sour cream

$1^1/2$ teaspoons vanilla extract

Seeds of 1 vanilla bean (see note)

$1^1/3$ cups cake flour ($5^1/4$ ounces)

$3/4$ teaspoon baking powder

$1/4$ teaspoon salt

GARNISH

Fresh berries
Whipped cream
Mint sprigs

1. For sauce, puree raspberries and strawberries in food processor or blender. Add sugar, cinnamon and vanilla. Push sauce through a fine wire mesh strainer into a bowl to remove seeds. Refrigerate overnight.

2. Heat oven to 350 degrees. Grease and flour an 8-by-4-inch loaf pan. Line bottom and sides of pan with parchment paper.

3. Beat butter in large bowl of electric mixer until light; beat in sugar until fluffy. Beat in eggs, one at a time. Beat in sour cream, vanilla extract and vanilla seeds. Sift together flour, baking powder and salt. Add to butter mixture; mix just until blended.

4. Spoon batter into prepared pan. Bake until a wooden pick inserted in center comes out clean, 50 to 60 minutes. Cool on wire rack about 20 minutes; unmold; cool completely.

5. To serve, cut cake into $1/2$-inch-thick slices. Pour sauce on each serving plate. Top with cake slice. Garnish with berries, whipped cream and a mint sprig.

Note: To obtain seeds from vanilla bean, split bean lengthwise in half; use the tip of a paring knife to scrape the tiny seeds into the batter. The bean can be saved for making vanilla sugar (page 99) and flavoring custards.

NUTS

KIPFERL (HAZELNUT CRESCENTS)

Kipferl (kip-fur-uhl) means crescent in German, and is the name of these fine holiday hazelnut cookies from columnist Peter Kump. They also are delicious made with pecans.

Preparation time: 35 minutes
Cooking time: 15 minutes
Yield: 5 to 6 dozen cookies

---

1 cup shelled hazelnuts (filberts)

$1/3$ cup granulated sugar

1 cup (2 sticks) unsalted butter, cut into 16 pieces, chilled

$1/2$ teaspoon vanilla extract

2 $1/4$ cups unsifted all-purpose flour

Pinch salt

Granulated or confectioners' sugar for top of cookies

1. Heat the oven to 350 degrees. Spread the hazelnuts on a baking sheet and bake about 15 minutes. Cool; as soon as they are cool enough to handle but still warm, rub them briskly in a clean towel to remove the skins.

2. Place the skinned nuts in a food processor with half the sugar and process into a fine powder, about 1 to 2 minutes. Add the butter, the remaining sugar and vanilla and process until smooth and well blended.

3. Sift the flour and salt together onto the butter mixture; mix until a dough forms.

4. Take a heaping teaspoon of the dough and roll it between your palms into a cigar shape, then gently bend it to form a small crescent about $1/2$ inches long. Repeat with the remaining dough. Place the crescents on a baking sheet.

5. Bake about 15 minutes. Cool slightly on a wire rack. Coat with granulated or confectioners' sugar. When completely cool, store the crescents in an airtight container; they will stay fresh for several weeks.

*The nuts for this tart can be varied to anything available, even peanuts,
but this version offers an elegant taste combination for entertaining.
If only salted nuts are available, simply drop them into boiling water, drain
and pat dry on paper towels before using.*

Preparation time: 45 minutes
Chilling time: 1 hour
Cooking time: 45 minutes
Yield: 10 to 14 servings

SWEET TART PASTRY

2¼ cups all-purpose flour

½ cup granulated sugar

½ teaspoon salt

¾ cup (1½ sticks) unsalted butter, cold, cut into pieces

3 egg yolks

3 tablespoons half-and-half

1 tablespoon vanilla extract

FILLING

2 cups each: dry-roasted unsalted cashews, blanched hazelnuts

2 cups packed light brown sugar

½ cup (1 stick) unsalted butter

5 tablespoons light corn syrup

⅓ cup whipping cream

HAZELNUT CREAM

1 cup whipping cream

2 tablespoons Frangelica (hazelnut-flavored liqueur)

1. For sweet tart pastry, put flour, sugar and salt into food processor. Process until mixed. Add butter. Process with on-off turns until mixture resembles coarse crumbs. Mix egg yolks, half-and-half and vanilla; add to food processor with motor running. Process just until mixture starts to form a ball. Remove to a sheet of wax paper and press dough together into a flat disk. Refrigerate until firm, about 30 minutes.

2. Heat oven to 375 degrees. Roll dough between 2 sheets of floured wax paper to a 12-inch circle. Remove 1 sheet of wax paper. Gently fit dough into a 10-inch tart pan with removable bottom. Carefully remove paper and trim dough to top edge of pan. Refrigerate for 30 minutes.

3. Line dough with foil and fill with pie weights or dried beans. Bake 15 minutes. Remove foil and beans. Continue baking until golden, about 10 minutes more. Cool completely on wire rack.

4. For filling, arrange cashews and hazelnuts over bottom of cooled crust. Put brown sugar, butter, corn syrup and cream into a medium saucepan. Cook and stir until sugar dissolves and boils hard.

5. Pour hot filling over nuts. Bake until filling bubbles, 15 to 20 minutes. Cool completely on wire rack.

6. For hazelnut cream, beat cream in small mixer bowl until soft peaks form. Beat in liqueur. Serve tart cut into thin wedges with a dollop of the whipped cream.

*Frozen yogurt can be made easily at home if you have an ice cream machine.
This version gets its nutty flavor from three sources: chopped almonds,
almond extract and those crispy Italian cookies called amaretti.*

Preparation time: 25 minutes
Freezing time: 1 to 2 hours
Yield: About 1 quart

$1/2$ **cup milk**

1$1/4$ teaspoons unflavored gelatin

$1/2$ **cup sugar**

2 tablespoons light corn syrup

$1/4$ **teaspoon almond extract**

$1/8$ **teaspoon ground nutmeg**

4 ripe medium peaches, peeled, sliced

1 cup plain yogurt

1 cup coarsely crumbled amaretti cookies (see note)

$1/4$ **cup toasted, sliced almonds**

GARNISH

Amaretto liqueur, optional

Fresh peach slices

Mint sprigs

1. Put milk and gelatin into a medium non-aluminum saucepan. Let stand until gelatin is softened. Cook and stir over low heat until gelatin dissolves. Remove from heat. Stir in sugar, corn syrup, almond extract and nutmeg; set aside.

2. Finely chop sliced peaches in a blender or food processor fitted with a metal blade. Stir peaches into gelatin mixture. Stir in yogurt.

3. Freeze in an ice cream maker according to manufacturer's directions. When almost firm, fold in crumbled cookies and toasted almonds. Put into freezer until firm enough to scoop, about 20 minutes or up to several days.

4. Serve in small scoops sprinkled with liqueur if desired. Garnish with peach slices and mint sprigs.

Note: Amaretti cookies are crisp almond-flavored Italian macaroons. They are available at Italian markets and some supermarkets.

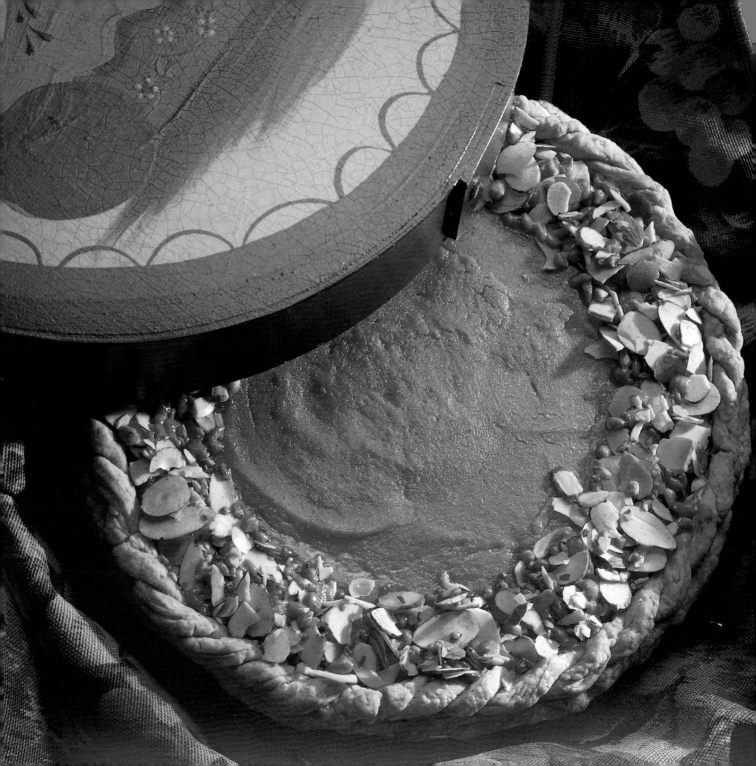

SWEET POTATO CANDY CRUNCH PIE

Sweet potato pie is a holiday tradition in many homes. This recipe adds a new twist: flavor and crunch from almond brickle bits, those toffee-like candies. See if you agree: It's the best!

Preparation time: 45 minutes
Cooking time: 55 minutes
Chilling time: 2 hours or overnight
Yield: 8 servings

3 medium sweet potatoes, about 1½ pounds

CRUST

½ cup almond brickle chips, such as Heath Bits O' Brickle

2 cups all-purpose flour

¾ teaspoon salt

6 tablespoons cold unsalted butter

⅓ cup cold vegetable shortening

4-6 tablespoons ice water

FILLING

1½ cups half-and-half

4 large eggs

¼ cup dark rum

⅓ cup each: packed dark brown sugar, granulated sugar

¼ cup melted butter

½ teaspoon each: freshly ground nutmeg, salt

⅛ teaspoon mace

TOPPING

⅓ cup almond brickle bits

¼ cup sliced unblanched almonds

Whipped cream for serving, if desired

1. Pierce potatoes in several places with tip of knife. Microwave on high, turning potatoes several times, until soft, 10 to 13 minutes. (Or, bake potatoes in a 350-degree oven until soft, about 1 hour.) Cool. Peel and mash slightly; there should be about 2½ cups.

2. For crust, put brickle chips into food processor or spice grinder. Process until finely crushed. Add flour and salt; process to mix. Add butter and shortening; process with on/off turns until mixture resembles coarse crumbs. Add 4 tablespoons cold water; process, adding more water as needed just until dough gathers into a ball. Shape into a disk and wrap tightly. Refrigerate at least 30 minutes.

3. Heat oven to 425 degrees. Roll out ⅔ of the dough on lightly floured work surface into an 11-inch circle. Fit into a 9-inch pie pan. Trim edge. Roll out remaining dough to ⅛-inch thickness. Cut into 1-inch wide strips and gently roll each strip into a rope. Twist two ropes together and position around edge of crust, pressing lightly so the rope adheres.

4. Line bottom of pie shell with foil. Fill with pie weights or dried beans. Bake until crust is light gold, about 10 minutes. Remove foil and pie weights. Cool on wire rack.

5. Reduce oven temperature to 350 degrees. For filling, put sweet potato pulp into food processor or blender. Add half-and-half, eggs, rum, sugars, butter, nutmeg, salt and mace. Process until smooth.

6. Pour filling into pie shell. Bake 35 minutes. Meanwhile, for topping, mix brickle bits and almonds in bowl. Remove pie from oven; sprinkle brickle mixture around outer edge. Continue baking until knife inserted in center is withdrawn clean, 20 minutes. Cool on rack.

7. Refrigerate at least 2 hours or overnight. Remove from refrigerator 30 minutes before serving. Top with whipped cream.

*This loaf cake recipe is adapted from one by Dennis and Gabrielle Kaniger,
who operate a stark, strikingly handsome restaurant called Venue in
Kansas City, Missouri.*

Preparation time: 40 minutes
Cooking time: 45 minutes
Yield: 8 to 10 servings

CAKE

¾ cup (1½ sticks) unsalted butter, softened

½ cup granulated sugar

2 large eggs

½ teaspoon vanilla extract

1½ cups cake flour

½ teaspoon each: baking soda, baking powder

¼ teaspoon salt

⅔ cup sour cream

½ cup blanched, ground hazelnuts

SAUCE

4 cups fresh raspberries

½ cup each: hazelnut-flavored liqueur, pure maple syrup

¼ cup (½ stick) unsalted butter

GARNISH

Raspberries or chopped hazelnuts

Whipped cream

1. Heat oven to 325 degrees. Grease a 9-by-5-inch loaf pan.

2. Beat butter and sugar with an electric mixer until smooth and light. Beat in eggs and vanilla. Sift together cake flour, baking soda, baking powder and salt. Add half the dry ingredients to the egg mixture. Add sour cream and then the remaining dry ingredients. Beat just until a smooth batter forms. Stir hazelnuts into the batter.

3. Pour batter into prepared pan. Smooth the top. Bake until a wooden pick inserted in the center comes out clean, about 45 minutes. Cool in pan on rack for 10 minutes. Turn out and let cool completely before slicing. (Cake may be wrapped and frozen.)

4. For the sauce, put raspberries, liqueur and maple syrup in a non-aluminum saucepan. Heat to a boil over medium heat. Boil for 5 minutes. Remove from heat and press through a fine wire mesh strainer into a bowl. Stir in butter until completely melted. Cool.

5. To serve, cut loaf cake into 1-inch slices. Lightly toast slices in an oven or toaster oven. Transfer to a dessert plate. Pour sauce over the cake and garnish with whipped cream and whole raspberries or hazelnuts. Alternatively, make a pool of sauce on the plate and top with a slice of cake and the garnish. Repeat as necessary.

NUTTY FRENCH TOAST DESSERT

This dessert, and the one on the next page, are from Pop's For Champagne, a Chicago champagne bar serving light fare that teams well with bubbly. Pick a champagne with some sweetness to match these recipes well.

Preparation time: 25 minutes
Cooking time: 30 minutes
Yield: 6 servings

NUT SYRUP

3 tablespoons butter

1 cup whole or coarsely chopped pecans

1 cup whole or coarsely chopped macadamia nuts

1 cup each: whipping cream, packed dark brown sugar

$1/3$ cup coffee-flavored liqueur

FRENCH TOAST

6 large eggs

$1/2$ cup each: extra-strong coffee, granulated sugar

1 cup whipping cream

1 tablespoon vanilla extract

12 slices ($1/2$-inch thick) French bread, preferably sourdough

3 tablespoons butter

6 small, barely ripe bananas, sliced thin

1. For nut syrup, melt butter in medium saucepan over medium heat. Add nuts and cook, stirring frequently, until lightly browned, about 3 minutes. Add cream, brown sugar and coffee liqueur to the pan. Stir to dissolve sugar, then cook over low heat until slightly thickened, about 15 minutes. Keep warm.

2. For French toast, beat eggs, coffee, granulated sugar, cream and vanilla together in shallow bowl. Dip bread slices in the batter for about 1 minute a side.

3. Heat 3 tablespoons butter in large skillet. When the butter bubbles, add soaked bread slices in single layer. Cook until golden brown on the bottom, about 3 minutes; turn and cook until second side browns.

4. Place 2 slices of French toast on each of 6 dessert plates. Top with sliced bananas and spoon warm nut sauce over all. Serve at once.

Another tasty treat from
Pop's For Champagne …

Preparation time: 45 minutes
Cooking time: 30 to 40 minutes
Chilling time: 1 hour or more
Yield: 10 to 12 servings

CAKE

2 medium-size ripe bananas, mashed, about 1 cup

2 tablespoons sour cream

2 large eggs

2 teaspoons grated lemon rind

1$\frac{1}{2}$ teaspoons vanilla extract

$\frac{1}{2}$ cup (1 stick) plus 2 tablespoons unsalted butter, softened

1 cup granulated sugar

2 cups all-purpose flour

1 teaspoon baking soda

$\frac{3}{4}$ teaspoon baking powder

$\frac{1}{2}$ teaspoon salt

ICING

8 ounces mascarpone cheese (see note)

2 teaspoons vanilla extract

2 cups confectioners' sugar

Pecans, chopped and whole

1. Heat oven to 350 degrees. Grease and flour a 9-inch springform pan.

2. For cake, puree bananas with sour cream, eggs, lemon rind and vanilla in food processor or blender. Set aside.

3. Beat butter and sugar together in large bowl of electric mixer until smooth and creamy. Sift flour together with baking soda, baking powder and salt. Alternately beat flour mixture and banana mixture into butter mixture in three additions until mixed.

4. Pour batter into prepared pan. Bake in middle of the oven until a tester or toothpick inserted into the center comes out clean, 30 to 40 minutes.

5. Cool on wire rack for 10 minutes. Remove sides and bottom of pan. Cool completely.

6. For icing, beat mascarpone in small bowl of electric mixer until smooth. Add vanilla and confectioners' sugar; beat until well mixed. If icing seems thin, refrigerate until thick enough to spread.

7. Spread icing over top and sides of cake. Use the palm of a hand to press chopped pecans onto sides. Decorate top outside edge with whole pecans. Refrigerate cake at least 1 hour. Remove from refrigerator 15 minutes before serving. To serve, cut into wedges.

Note: Mascarpone cheese is sold in specialty food stores and Italian markets. If mascarpone is unavailable, substitute softened cream cheese.

This pecan cake is an adaptation of a recipe by Elizabeth James, who has been farming pecans with her husband, George, for nearly half a century in Missouri.

Preparation time: 1 hour
Cooking time: 35 to 40 minutes
Yield: 10 to 12 servings

CAKE LAYERS

3 cups all-purpose flour

1 teaspoon baking soda

4 teaspoons unsweetened cocoa powder

1 cup (2 sticks) unsalted butter, softened

2 cups granulated sugar

5 large eggs, separated

1 cup buttermilk

5 teaspoons strong coffee

2 teaspoons vanilla extract

1 cup chopped pecans

PECAN FROSTING

1 cup (2 sticks) unsalted butter, softened

$3^1/_2$ cups confectioners' sugar

4 teaspoons unsweetened cocoa powder

$2^1/_2$ tablespoons strong coffee

1 tablespoon vanilla extract

1 cup chopped pecans

1. For cake, heat oven to 350 degrees. Grease two 9-inch round cake pans. Sift together flour, baking soda and cocoa powder; set aside.

2. Beat butter and sugar together in large bowl of electric mixer until very light and creamy smooth. Add the egg yolks and beat again.

3. Add the flour mixture alternately with the buttermilk in 3 additions. Stir in coffee and vanilla, then the pecans.

4. Beat egg whites in a clean bowl to soft peaks. Fold into cake batter gently but thoroughly. Pour batter equally into prepared pans. Smooth tops with a spatula until level.

5. Bake in middle of oven until cake center springs back when touched and wooden pick inserted in the center comes out clean, 35 to 40 minutes. Cool in the pans on wire racks for 10 minutes. Invert to unmold cakes from pans. Let cool completely on racks.

6. For pecan frosting, beat butter in large bowl of electric mixer until creamy. Add confectioners' sugar and cocoa, beating until mixed. Add coffee and vanilla and continue to beat until smooth and fluffy.

7. Frost between cake layers, then frost sides and top of stacked cake. Press chopped pecans onto sides of frosted cake with the palm of your hand.

This is a rich quick bread, chock-full of nuts and chocolate. Serve it as part of a sweet table or with tea or coffee. It is also ideal for gift-giving but you may want to make smaller loaves by spreading the batter into two 5³/4-by-3¹/4 inch loaf pans and reducing the baking time to 30 to 40 minutes. For the best results, use a high-quality semisweet chocolate broken into ¹/2-inch chunks rather than chocolate chips.

Preparation time: 25 minutes
Cooking time: 55 to 60 minutes
Yield: 1 loaf

1³/4 cups all-purpose flour

1 teaspoon baking soda

¹/2 teaspoon salt

¹/4 cup (¹/2 stick) unsalted butter, softened

¹/3 cup sugar

1 teaspoon vanilla extract

1 large egg

¹/2 cup unsweetened cocoa powder

2 teaspoons instant espresso powder

1 cup buttermilk

2 cups each: coarsely chopped walnuts, small chunks semi-sweet chocolate

1 cup raisins, optional

About ¹/4 cup coarsely chopped walnuts for top

1. Heat oven to 375 degrees. Butter and flour a 9-by-5-inch loaf pan. Sift the flour with the baking soda and salt.

2. Beat butter, sugar and vanilla in large bowl of electric mixer until light and creamy. Beat in egg until well mixed. Beat in cocoa and espresso powder. Alternately beat in flour mixture and buttermilk until moistened. Fold in 2 cups walnuts, chocolate chunks and raisins.

3. Transfer batter to prepared pan. Arrange walnut pieces over top of loaf. Bake until cake pulls away from sides of pan and wooden pick inserted in center comes out clean, 55 to 60 minutes. Cool on wire rack 10 minutes. Unmold; cool completely on wire rack.

ALMOND BUTTER COOKIES

These dainty cookies are good simply with coffee or tea, or as an accompaniment to a fruit dessert.

Preparation time: 45 minutes
Chilling time: 2 hours or more
Cooking time: 10 minutes
Yield: About 4 dozen

---

1 cup (2 sticks) unsalted butter, softened

1 cup sugar

1/4 teaspoon almond extract

1 large egg

1 can (8 ounces) almond paste

1 1/2 cups sifted all-purpose flour

1/2 teaspoon baking powder

1/4 teaspoon each: baking soda, salt

Sugar for rolling

Sliced almonds

1. Beat butter, sugar and almond extract in large bowl of electric mixer until light and fluffy. Beat in egg and almond paste; beat thoroughly to incorporate almond paste. Add sifted dry ingredients; beat until blended. Refrigerate dough until cold, 2 hours or more.

2. Heat oven to 350 degrees. Using about 2 teaspoons of dough for each cookie, shape dough into balls. Roll balls in granulated sugar. Place on ungreased baking sheets. Flatten slightly with the bottom of a glass that has been dipped in sugar. Press a few almond slices into top of each cookie. Bake until delicately browned, 8 to 10 minutes. Transfer to wire rack to cool. Store in an airtight tin.

Preparing the layers for these cookie-bars is well worth the time. The recipe combines all the things we love in one rich dessert.

Preparation time: 40 minutes
Cooking time: 45 minutes
Yield: 50 1½-inch squares

FIRST LAYER

4 ounces semisweet chocolate, coarsely chopped

¾ cup granulated sugar

½ cup (1 stick) unsalted butter, softened

2 large eggs

2 teaspoons vanilla extract

½ cup all-purpose flour

⅛ teaspoon salt

SECOND LAYER

¼ cup (½ stick) unsalted butter

¾ cup packed light brown sugar

2 tablespoons all-purpose flour

2 large eggs, lightly beaten

2 teaspoons vanilla extract

3 cups pecan halves

THIRD LAYER

4 ounces semisweet chocolate, coarsely chopped

½ cup (1 stick) unsalted butter

1. Line a 9-inch square pan with aluminum foil and butter the foil. For the first layer, melt the chocolate in the top of a double boiler. Or, melt in the microwave oven on medium (50 percent) power in an uncovered glass bowl. Set aside to cool slightly.

2. Beat the butter and sugar in large bowl of electric mixer until smooth and light, about 2 minutes. Add the eggs, one at a time, mixing well after each addition. Add the chocolate and vanilla and mix well; fold in the flour.

3. Transfer batter to prepared pan, spreading it in an even layer. Place pan in freezer while you prepare the next layer. Heat oven to 325 degrees.

4. For the second layer, melt butter in a small pan. Add the brown sugar and cook over low heat until smooth. Stir in the flour and cook 30 seconds longer. Remove from heat and cool slightly. When mixture has cooled a bit, take a small spoonful and stir into the beaten eggs. Then, whisking as you do so, add egg mixture to the rest of the brown sugar mixture. Add pecans and vanilla and mix well.

5. Pour pecan layer over chilled chocolate layer. Bake until a toothpick inserted in the center of the chocolate layer comes out almost clean, about 45 minutes. When properly baked, there still should be a few moist crumbs on the pick. Transfer to a wire rack and cool completely.

6. For the third layer, melt chocolate and butter, whisking so the butter is completely mixed into chocolate. Pour over cooled bars, tipping pan so the entire surface is evenly coated (see note). Refrigerate at least 2 hours or up to 5 days before serving. To serve, cut into small squares.

Note: If desired, the melted chocolate and butter for the third layer can be drizzled over the bars in a decorative pattern instead of used to coat the entire surface.

TOASTED PISTACHIO CHOCOLATE TORTE

Toasting nuts before using them in desserts brings out their full flavor. Try to find natural pistachios. In addition to not being dyed, they often are fresher. This cake is also delicious when frosted with chocolate or vanilla buttercream.

Preparation time: 45 minutes
Cooking time: 30 to 40 minutes
Yield: One 9-inch cake

---

4 ounces shelled natural (undyed) unsalted pistachio nuts

4 ounces semisweet chocolate

1/3 cup all-purpose flour, sifted

1/4 cup unsweetened cocoa powder, sifted

1/2 cup (1 stick) unsalted butter, softened

1/2 cup granulated sugar

1 teaspoon vanilla extract

4 large eggs, separated

Pinch salt

Red currant jelly or seedless raspberry jam

Confectioners' sugar

Fresh raspberries

1. Heat oven to 300 degrees. Butter and flour a 9-inch springform pan. Put nuts into a baking pan. Bake until lightly toasted and fragrant, about 10 minutes. Cool. Chop very finely or put into food processor and process with on/off turns until finely ground.

2. Chop chocolate very finely or put into food processor and process with on/off turns until very finely chopped, almost powdery. Mix nuts, chocolate, flour and cocoa in small bowl.

3. Beat butter and 1/4 cup of the granulated sugar in large bowl of electric mixer until light and creamy. Beat in vanilla extract. Beat in egg yolks, one at a time, until light. Add chocolate mixture; stir lightly until blended.

4. Beat egg whites and salt in large bowl of electric mixer until foamy. Beat in remaining 1/4 cup sugar until stiff – but not dry – peaks form. Gently stir 1/4 of the whites into the butter mixture to lighten it. Fold in remaining whites. Do not overmix.

5. Spread batter into prepared pan. Bake until top springs back when lightly touched and cake has pulled away from sides of pan, 30 to 40 minutes. Cool on wire rack 15 minutes. Remove sides of pan; invert onto wire rack; remove bottom of pan; cool cake completely on wire rack.

6. Heat jelly or jam until warm and liquid; brush generously over top and sides of cake. Sprinkle generously with confectioners' sugar. Garnish with fresh raspberries.

FRUITS

Cobblers can be made several hours in advance of serving but are best served the same day. If transporting a cobbler to a picnic or summer party, bake it early enough to allow it to cool. Then cover loosely with aluminum foil and keep it level during the trip. Cake flour makes this dough very tender.

Preparation time: 45 minutes
Cooking time: 40 minutes
Yield: 6 servings

COBBLER DOUGH

Rind of 1 small orange

$1/4$ cup sugar

$1^1/2$ cups cake flour or $1^1/4$ cups all-purpose flour

$1^3/4$ teaspoons baking powder

Pinch salt

$1/4$ cup each: cold unsalted butter, cold regular margarine

$1/3$ cup half-and-half or whole milk

PLUM-BERRY FILLING

6 ripe assorted plums

1 cup blueberries

$1/2$ pint small strawberries, hulled, halved

$1/2$ pint red raspberries or blackberries

3 tablespoons cornstarch

2 tablespoons fresh orange juice

$1/3$ to $1/2$ cup sugar to taste

NUT TOPPING

$1/4$ cup sliced almonds

Vanilla sugar, see page 99

Vanilla ice cream or whipped cream for serving

1. For cobbler dough, remove rind from orange (colored part only) with a vegetable peeler. Put rind into food processor; add sugar; process until rind is very finely minced. Add flour, baking powder and salt; process to mix. Cut butter and margarine into pieces; add to processor. Process with on/off turns until mixture resembles coarse crumbs. Add half-and-half; process just until dough gathers into clumps.

2. Turn dough out onto a floured piece of wax paper. Gather into a flat disk (dough is very soft). Sprinkle lightly with flour and wrap in the wax paper. Refrigerate 20 to 30 minutes.

3. Heat oven to 350 degrees. Generously butter an 8-inch-square (or other shallow 5-cup capacity) oven-to-table baking dish.

4. For filling, cut plums in half; remove pits. Cut into $1/4$-inch-thick slices. Put into bowl; add berries, cornstarch, orange juice and sugar to taste. Toss to mix well. Transfer mixture to prepared dish.

5. Unwrap dough and place on floured wax paper; top with a second sheet of floured wax paper. Roll gently until the same size as the baking dish. Remove top sheet of paper. Invert dough over fruit filling. Carefully peel away wax paper. (Do not worry if dough doesn't look perfect; it spreads slightly during baking.) Sprinkle with almonds; gently press into dough; sprinkle generously with vanilla sugar.

6. Bake until dough is golden and fruit is bubbly, 35 to 40 minutes. Cool on wire rack at least 2 hours. Serve warm or at room temperature with scoops of ice cream or whipped cream.

Garnishing and presentation take on heightened importance for dessert buffets. This doesn't mean that everything needs to have the signature look of a professional. Special flourishes can be very simple yet still carry high impact. The cheesecake can be crowned with a selection of summer's best and brightest fruits. Fresh garden flowers and greens can be used to spiff up platters and serving trays.

Preparation time: 40 minutes
Cooking time: 45 minutes
Yield: One 10-inch cake, 12 servings

CRUST

4 ounces butter cookie crumbs

1/2 cup pecan or walnut halves

1/4 cup melted unsalted butter

1/8 teaspoon freshly grated nutmeg

FILLING

3 large eggs

1 1/4 cups sugar

4 packages (8 ounces each) cream cheese

2 tablespoons orange-flavored liqueur

TOPPING

Fresh berries, such as blueberries, raspberries and strawberries

1/4 cup currant jelly, melted

Raspberry sauce, see page 97, optional

1. Heat oven to 350 degrees. Have a 10-inch springform pan ready.

2. For the crust, crush the cookies and nuts in a food processor. Add the melted butter and nutmeg and process to combine. Press evenly over bottom of pan. Bake until set, about 12 minutes.

3. For the filling, wipe out the processor work bowl. Process the eggs and sugar until smooth, 1 minute. Add the cream cheese and liqueur; process until completely smooth, 1 to 2 minutes, scraping down the sides of the bowl as necessary. Pour into crust.

4. Bake cake just until it is set at the edges, 33 to 35 minutes. It will be somewhat soft and jiggly in the center. Transfer to a wire rack and cool completely; refrigerate several hours or overnight.

5. For the topping, arrange the berries over top of cake as desired. Brush with melted currant jelly. Serve slices of the cake topped with raspberry sauce, if you like.

*Probably the best way to enjoy apricots is to eat them fresh, out of hand.
However, should an overabundance of fresh fruit find its way to your kitchen,
this apricot-strawberry pie provides a delightfully different way to use the excess.*

Preparation time: 1 hour
Chilling time: 1 hour
Cooking time: 40 to 45 minutes
Yield: One 9-inch pie

PIE DOUGH

2 cups all-purpose flour

$3/4$ teaspoon salt

$2/3$ cup chilled vegetable shortening or lard

2 tablespoons chilled butter

4 to 5 tablespoons ice water

FILLING

$2^1/2$ pounds fresh apricots

$1^1/2$ cups halved strawberries

$1/3$ cup plus 2 tablespoons sugar

3 tablespoons cornstarch

2 tablespoons fresh lemon juice

$1/4$ teaspoon freshly grated nutmeg

1 tablespoon butter, melted

1 egg mixed with 1 tablespoon whipping cream

Creme fraiche, see page 99, or whipped cream, optional

1. For pie dough, mix flour and salt in large bowl. Cut in shortening and butter with pastry blender or two knives until mixture resembles coarse crumbs. Using a fork, stir in ice water just until mixture gathers easily into a ball. Wrap dough in plastic and refrigerate at least 1 hour.

2. Roll out half the dough on a lightly floured surface to $1/8$-inch thickness. Fit into a 9-inch pie pan. Trim edge. Refrigerate.

3. Roll out remaining dough into a $1/8$-inch-thick rectangle. Cut into $1/2$-inch-wide strips using a fluted pastry wheel. Arrange strips in lattice fashion on a cookie sheet lined with wax paper. Refrigerate.

4. Heat oven to 425 degrees. For filling, put apricots into a large pot of boiling water. Boil for 30 seconds. Drain; rinse under cold water to stop the cooking. Peel apricots. Remove pits and cut fruit into quarters.

5. Put apricots, strawberries, $1/3$ cup of the sugar, cornstarch, lemon juice and nutmeg into large bowl. Toss to mix. Spoon into pastry-lined pie pan. Drizzle with melted butter. Carefully slide lattice top over fruit. Press lattice strips into edges of pie shell. Moisten with water if needed. Flute edges.

6. Put pie onto a baking sheet. Brush lattice strips with egg-cream mixture. Sprinkle with 2 tablespoons of the sugar. Bake at 425 degrees for 25 minutes. Reduce oven temperature to 375 degrees. Continue baking until strips are golden, 15 to 20 minutes. Cool completely on wire rack. Serve pie with a dollop of creme fraiche or whipped cream, if you like.

A true convenience dessert, this recipe for apricot dumplings is quick and easy. It can be varied as you like, using fresh fruit, peeled and pitted, when it is in season. Peaches are a natural substitute, but canned pears work well, too.

Preparation time: 10 minutes
Cooking time: 25 minutes
Yield: 4 servings

---

1 can (30 ounces) halved apricots or peaches

$1/2$ cup packed light brown sugar

1 teaspoon cinnamon

Pinch freshly ground nutmeg

2 cups buttermilk baking mix, such as Bisquick

$2/3$ cup milk

Pinch each: salt, granulated sugar

Half-and-half, whipped cream or vanilla ice cream for topping

1. Combine apricots and their liquid with brown sugar, cinnamon and nutmeg in large, heavy skillet or saucepan. Heat to boil and cook until slightly thickened, about 5 minutes.

2. Meanwhile, mix buttermilk baking mix, milk, salt and granulated sugar in bowl. Drop mixture by large spoonfuls evenly over apricots. Cover and cook 10 minutes. Uncover; cook until dumplings are cooked through, about 10 more minutes. Spoon into serving bowls and top with half-and-half, whipped cream or ice cream.

INDIVIDUAL HOT APPLE TARTS

A dinner party finale can be made special by serving guests their very own individual tarts. The pastry for the following tart is very rich and delicate. It should be made with chilled ingredients and worked as briefly as possible.

Preparation time: 1 hour
Chilling time: 2 hours or more
Cooking time: 20 minutes
Yield: 8 servings

CRUST

1½ cups all-purpose flour

2 tablespoons granulated sugar

Pinch salt

¾ cup (1½ sticks) cold unsalted butter

2 to 3 tablespoons cold water

FILLING

3 to 4 firm apples, such as Jonathan, peeled, quartered, cored

⅓ cup apricot jam or preserves, heated

⅓ cup granulated sugar

4 tablespoons butter, cut into very small pieces

TOPPING

4 ounces cream cheese

¾ cup whipping cream

2 tablespoons superfine sugar

1. For crust, put flour, sugar and salt into a bowl. Cut in butter until mixture resembles coarse crumbs. Sprinkle with water. Stir quickly with spoon for a few turns, then finish with your hands to form a ball of dough. Wrap in wax paper and refrigerate about 15 minutes.

2. Cut dough in half. Rewrap one piece and return it to the refrigerator. Roll out the other piece to a round about 13 inches in diameter. Cut out four 4½-inch circles with a chilled cookie cutter. Transfer each circle to an ungreased baking sheet, using a chilled spatula. Repeat with remaining dough, placing these rounds on a second baking sheet. Refrigerate.

3. For filling, cut apples into ¼-inch-thick slices. Brush jam over chilled pastry circles. Place overlapping slices of apple on top of the jam, covering each circle completely.

Sprinkle with sugar and dot with butter bits. Chill tarts at least 2 hours, or until ready to bake. (Apples will darken somewhat during chilling period. If desired, toss slices in lemon juice before arranging on pastry rounds.)

4. For topping, beat cream cheese in small bowl of electric mixer until fluffy. Slowly beat in cream, then sugar. The topping should have the consistency of whipped cream. Place in a serving dish; refrigerate.

5. Heat oven to 475 degrees. About 25 minutes before you wish to serve dessert, place tarts on baking sheets in the oven. Bake for 5 minutes, then reduce oven temperature to 400 degrees. Continue baking tarts until the edges are golden, 10 to 15 additional minutes. Remove from oven. Preheat broiler.

6. Brush warm jam over baked tarts. Then broil tarts, 6 inches from heat source, until deep gold, about 2 minutes. Transfer tarts to individual serving plates. Offer topping at the table.

LIGHT CHERRY BRUNCH BARS

These brunch bars devised by Jeanne Jones have about a third fewer calories and half the fat of most bar cookies.

Preparation time: 25 minutes
Baking time: 30 minutes
Yield: 15 servings

2 tablespoons cornstarch

$^1/_3$ cup water

1 can (16 ounces) tart pie cherries, packed in water

$1^1/_3$ cups sugar

5 egg whites

$^1/_2$ cup (1 stick) corn-oil margarine, softened

1 whole egg

$^1/_2$ cup buttermilk

1 teaspoon vanilla extract

3 cups unbleached all-purpose flour

$1^1/_2$ teaspoons baking powder

$^1/_4$ teaspoon salt

1. Heat oven to 350 degrees. Dissolve cornstarch in water. Strain liquid from cherries into saucepan. Add $^1/_3$ cup of the sugar; cook and stir over low heat until sugar is dissolved. Add cherries and cornstarch mixture; cook and stir until thickened, 3 to 4 minutes. Remove from heat.

2. Beat egg whites in large bowl of electric mixer until stiff but not dry; set aside. In another bowl, beat margarine and remaining 1 cup sugar until light. Gradually beat in whole egg and buttermilk, then vanilla. Combine dry ingredients and add to creamed mixture; fold in beaten egg whites.

3. Spread two-thirds of the batter over bottom of a 15-by-10-inch jellyroll pan sprayed with non-stick vegetable spray. Spread with cherry mixture and drop spoonfuls of remaining batter on top. Bake until batter is golden, about 30 minutes. Cool on wire rack. Serve cut in squares or diamonds.

The tart filling of lemon meringue pie gets a touch of creaminess from sour cream in columnist Abby Mandel's version of this American classic.

Preparation time: 45 minutes
Baking time: 31 to 33 minutes
Yield: One 9-inch pie

FILLING

**Rind (colored part only) of
1 lemon, removed with a zester or
grater**

1⅓ cups sugar

4 large eggs

¼ cup sour cream

**½ cup (1 stick) unsalted butter,
melted**

½ cup fresh lemon juice

Prebaked 9-inch pie shell

MERINGUE TOPPING

5 large egg whites

¼ teaspoon cream of tartar

1 cup sugar

1. Fifteen minutes before baking, place the rack in the center of the oven and heat oven to 375 degrees.

2. For filling, mince the lemon rind with the sugar in a food processor so it is as fine as possible. Add eggs, sour cream and butter and process for 1 minute, stopping once to scrape down the sides of the bowl. Add the lemon juice and mix 5 seconds. (Filling also can be made with a blender and electric mixer: Mince the lemon rind with the sugar in a blender so it is as fine as possible; put the minced lemon rind and sugar in the large bowl of an electric mixer; add the eggs and butter. Mix on high speed until thick; add the sour cream and mix until smooth. Reduce to low speed and add the lemon juice.)

3. Pour the filling into the prebaked pastry. Bake until filling is slightly soft in the center, about 25 minutes. It will set up more as it cools. Cool to room temperature on a wire rack. Can be made a day in advance to this point and refrigerated. Bring to room temperature before adding meringue.

4. For the meringue, heat the oven to 425 degrees. Beat the egg whites in large bowl of electric mixer on medium until foamy. Add the cream of tartar and beat on high until they hold soft peaks. Gradually add the sugar, beating well after each addition. Continue to beat until meringue is thick and shiny.

5. Spread the meringue over the pie, mounding it in the center. Use the back of a spoon to make peaks and swirls. Immediately bake just until lightly browned, 6 to 8 minutes. The pie is best served shortly after the meringue is added but can be held up to 3 hours.

Poached pears in wine is a favorite recipe of Walt and Tina Dreyer, owners of Grand Cru, a small Sonoma County winery. Although they usually sip white zinfandel as an aperitif, they have found its slight sweetness is perfect for this recipe.

Preparation time: 20 minutes
Cooking time: 25 minutes
Yield: 8 servings

¼ cup lemon juice

Cold water

8 pears, Bosc preferred

1 bottle (750 ml) white zinfandel wine (see note)

1 cup sugar

4 whole cloves

1 bay leaf

½ vanilla bean

Mint sprigs, whipped cream or raspberry puree

1. Mix lemon juice and enough cold water to cover the pears in a large bowl. Peel pears. Using a melon baller or a small spoon, core pears from the bottom, leaving them whole, and place them in the water to soak.

2. Put wine, sugar, cloves, bay leaf and vanilla bean in a pan large enough to hold the pears in a single layer. Heat to a boil, stirring occasionally to dissolve sugar. Add the pears, and adjust heat to a bare simmer. Place a wax-paper circle cut to fit the pan over the pears. Cover the pan. Poach until tender, 10 to 20 minutes depending on ripeness.

3. Remove pears from cooking liquid and refrigerate. Boil cooking liquid until reduced by half. Refrigerate the liquid until cold.

4. To serve, spoon a small amount of syrup into shallow bowls or plates. Place a pear upright in each bowl. Garnish with mint, whipped cream or raspberry puree.

Note: This recipe also may be made with gewurztraminer.

PASSION FRUIT MOUSSE IN PHYLLO BASKETS

Celeste Zeccola, pastry chef at Carlos restaurant in Highland Park, Illinois, created this smashing dessert for Valentine's Day, but it also is worthy of any dinner party.

Preparation time: 1 hour
Chilling time: Several hours
Cooking time: 15 minutes
Yield: 4 servings

MOUSSE

1 teaspoon unflavored gelatin

3 tablespoons cold water

10 passion fruit or $\frac{1}{2}$ cup fresh lemon juice

$\frac{1}{4}$ cup each: fresh orange juice, granulated sugar

3 large egg yolks

$\frac{3}{4}$ cup whipping cream, whipped to soft peaks

PHYLLO BASKETS

2 sheets phyllo dough

3 tablespoons melted butter

4 teaspoons confectioners' sugar

RASPBERRY CREME ANGLAISE

$\frac{1}{2}$ cup granulated sugar

4 large egg yolks

1 cup whole milk

$\frac{3}{4}$ cup fresh raspberries

Fresh raspberries, red candy hearts, optional

1. For mousse, sprinkle gelatin over cold water; let stand until softened. If using passion fruit, cut in half and scoop pulp into a wire mesh strainer set over a bowl. Push pulp through the strainer to remove the seeds.

2. Measure $\frac{1}{2}$ cup of the passion fruit juice or lemon juice. Whisk juice with orange juice, sugar and egg yolks in the top of a double boiler. Place over simmering water. Cook, stirring often, until slightly thickened, about 15 minutes. Do not boil. Remove top pan and add gelatin mixture, stirring to dissolve. Refrigerate just until the mixture thickens but has not begun to set, 30 to 45 minutes. Gently fold in whipped cream; refrigerate until set, about 1 hour or up to 2 days.

3. For phyllo baskets, heat oven to 425 degrees. Brush each sheet of phyllo with melted butter and sprinkle lightly with confectioners' sugar. Stack sheets together. With sharp knife or pizza cutter, cut into $\frac{1}{2}$-inch strips. Weave together as for a lattice pie crust and carefully set into 4 small, deep oven-proof bowls, muffin tins or popover pans.

Bake until crisp and golden, 12 to 15 minutes. Remove from bowls and cool on wire rack. Baskets can be made days in advance and stored at room temperature in a tin.

4. For raspberry creme Anglaise, whisk egg yolks with half of the sugar. Put remaining half of sugar in a medium pan with milk and heat to a boil. Whisk several tablespoons of the hot milk into the yolk mixture. Then whisk the yolk mixture into the rest of the milk in the pan. Cook over medium heat, stirring constantly, until mixture thickens enough to coat the back of a wooden spoon, 7 to 8 minutes. Do not let the mixture boil or it will curdle. Remove from heat. Smash berries and add them to sauce. The sauce should be deep pink; add more berries if necessary to deepen color. Strain and refrigerate until serving, as long as 2 days.

5. Fill each basket with mousse. Place on a dessert plate and spoon sauce around it. Garnish with raspberries and candy hearts.

Columnist William Rice came up with a new version of peach pie for an article he wrote on pies. "Can less be more?" he wrote about this recipe. "Try for yourself and find out."

Preparation time: 45 minutes
Cooking time: 20 minutes
Yield: 6 servings

SHORTBREAD

½ cup (1 stick) unsalted butter or margarine, softened

¼ cup confectioners' sugar

2 ounces reduced-calorie Neufchatel cream cheese

⅔ cup all-purpose flour

½ cup cake flour

¼ teaspoon each: baking soda, salt

TOPPING

6 ounces Neufchatel cream cheese

½ cup confectioners' sugar

1 tablespoon kirsch

FILLING

6 medium peaches

3 tablespoons butter or margarine

1½ tablespoons each: granulated sugar, kirsch

¾ teaspoon vanilla extract

1. For shortbread, heat oven to 350 degrees. Beat butter, confectioners' sugar and cream cheese in large bowl of electric mixer until creamy. Add both flours, baking soda and salt; mix only until blended into a dough. Do not overmix.

2. Place dough on a lightly floured surface and push or roll out into a ¼-inch-thick circle. Use a 3-inch round cookie cutter to cut the dough into at least 6 rounds, reforming dough scraps as necessary.

3. Transfer rounds to an ungreased baking sheet. Pierce lightly with a fork. Bake until just beginning to color, about 15 minutes. Cool on a wire rack and set aside. (Shortbread may be made in advance. Store in a cookie tin.)

4. For topping, blend cream cheese, confectioners' sugar and kirsch until smooth. Set aside at room temperature. (Topping may be made in advance. Cover and refrigerate but bring back to room temperature before serving.)

5. For filling, drop peaches into boiling water for 30 seconds to loosen skins, then peel. Cut each peach into thin wedges.

6. Heat butter in a large skillet. Add peach slices, sugar to taste, kirsch and vanilla. Cook and stir until peaches are just heated through, 3 to 4 minutes. Pour contents of skillet into a strainer set over a bowl. Return juices that collect in the bowl to the skillet and boil to reduce them to a syrup consistency. Remove skillet from heat, return peach slices to syrup and stir to blend.

7. To serve, place 1 shortbread round on each serving plate. Spoon warm peaches onto the shortbreads, then spoon 1 rounded tablespoon of topping over the peaches. Serve immediately.

Columnist Jeanne Jones says the only trick in making this cloudlike dessert is to have the milk and a stainless steel bowl very cold before using them. The mousse makes a fine topping for fruit salad, too. Each serving has only 130 calories.

Preparation time: 25 minutes
Chilling time: 2 hours
Yield: 5 servings

1 envelope unflavored gelatin

3 tablespoons cool water

1 tablespoon grated lemon rind

1 teaspoon grated lime rind

¼ cup each: freshly squeezed lemon juice, lime juice

6 tablespoons sugar

1 can (12 ounces) evaporated skim milk, cold

10 lemon leaves for garnish, if available

1. Soften gelatin in the cool water in small dish; set aside.

2. Put lemon and lime rinds in small pan. Cover with water. Heat to boil. Strain and set rinds aside.

3. Combine lemon and lime juices in a non-aluminum saucepan. Add sugar and heat to boil. Remove from heat and add gelatin and mix until gelatin is completely dissolved. Add lemon and lime rinds, mix well and set aside.

4. Whip cold canned milk in a chilled bowl with chilled beaters until soft peaks form. Fold juice mixture into whipped milk. Spoon 1 cup into each of 5 ramekins or sherbet glasses and refrigerate until cold and set, about 2 hours.

5. To serve, garnish each serving with lemon leaves if available.

BLUEBERRY MORNING CAKE

"To me, this is the perfect kind of cake," said Chelsea Williams, a talented Missouri baker. "It's unadorned, not too sweet and moist with berries. It keeps well and gets better with age." This recipe makes two cakes, one to eat now and one to freeze for later.

Preparation time: 45 minutes
Cooking time: 65 minutes
Yield: One Bundt cake and
one loaf cake

---

1 pound unsalted butter, softened

3 cups granulated sugar

6 large eggs

2 teaspoons lemon extract or grated rind of 2 lemons

4 cups unbleached all-purpose flour

1 tablespoon baking powder

$1/2$ teaspoon salt

1 cup milk

$2^1/2$ cups fresh blueberries

1. Heat oven to 350 degrees. Grease an 8-by-4-inch loaf pan and a 12-cup Bundt pan.

2. Beat butter and sugar together in large bowl of electric mixer until very well blended. Beat in eggs, one at a time, beating well after each addition. Add extract or lemon rind and stir. Set aside. Sift together all but 2 tablespoons of the flour, baking powder and salt into a separate bowl.

3. Alternately beat flour mixture and milk into butter mixture in 3 additions beginning and ending with flour. Toss blueberries with remaining 2 tablespoons flour. Fold blueberries into batter.

4. Transfer 2 cups of the batter into prepared loaf pan. Transfer remaining batter into prepared Bundt pan. Smooth with a spatula to level the surfaces.

5. Bake the cakes until a wooden pick inserted in center comes out clean, about 45 minutes for the loaf pan and 65 minutes for the Bundt pan.

6. Remove from the oven and cool on wire racks for 10 minutes before inverting to unmold cakes. Cool completely on wire racks.

PEAR FRANGIPANE TART

Make sure when you cut this open-faced pie that each serving gets a slice with a pear.

Preparation time: 45 minutes
Baking time: 35 minutes
Yield: 6 to 8 servings

1 unbaked pie crust, for 9- or 10-inch pie

FRANGIPANE

$^1/_2$ of an 8-ounce can almond paste

$^1/_4$ cup sugar

2 large eggs

1 tablespoon all-purpose flour

FILLING

1 can (29 ounces) pear halves

2 tablespoons apricot preserves, melted, strained

1. Heat oven to 450 degrees. Fit dough into 9- or 10-inch tart pan with removable bottom.

2. For frangipane, beat almond paste and sugar in bowl of electric mixer until soft. Beat in eggs one at a time. Scrape down sides of bowl after each egg. Beat in flour.

3. For filling, spread frangipane over dough in pan. Drain pears and pat dry. Slice halves into $^1/_4$-inch thick slices, but keep pear shape. Lift halves onto frangipane and place stem end pointing to the center. Fan sliced pears slightly outward.

4. Bake 15 minutes. Reduce oven temperature to 350 degrees and bake until puffed and golden brown, about 20 minutes. Brush pears with melted preserves while still warm. Cool on wire rack.

The cranberries give color and tang to this festive pie. A lattice top with leaves makes the perfect presentation.

Preparation time: 45 minutes
Baking time: 45 minutes
Yield: 6 to 8 servings

---

3 large tart apples, such as Granny Smith, peeled, cored, sliced

1 bag (12 ounces) cranberries

$1/2$ cup sugar

Juice of $1/2$ lemon

1 tablespoon cornstarch

$1/2$ teaspoon ground cinnamon

Grated rind of 1 orange

Pie dough for double crust 9-inch pie, chilled

3 tablespoons butter

1. Heat oven to 425 degrees. Mix apples, cranberries, sugar, lemon juice, cornstarch, cinnamon and orange rind in large bowl.

2. Divide chilled dough into 2 portions, one slightly larger than the other. Chill smaller portion until ready to roll out.

3. For bottom crust, place larger portion on floured board or work surface. Roll with quick strokes of rolling pin, working away from the center to make a circle 1 inch larger than top of pie pan and about $1/8$-inch thick.

4. Fold dough and lift into 9-inch pie pan. Unfold and fit lightly into pan. Trim edge with scissors or sharp knife, allowing about an extra $1/2$ inch to hang over edge.

5. Gently heap filling high in the center. Cut butter into small pieces and scatter over filling.

6. For top crust, roll out reserved dough as for bottom crust (see note). Seal and crimp edges.

7. Bake 15 minutes. Reduce oven temperature to 350 degrees. Bake until crust is golden brown, filling is bubbly and apples are tender, about 30 minutes longer.

Note: For lattice top, cut dough into $1/2$-inch wide strips with fluted pastry wheel. Place several strips of dough over filling, about 1 inch apart. Fold every other strip back toward center of pie. Place 1 strip of dough crosswise on top of strips that were not folded. Unfold strips. Now fold back strips that are covered by the crosswise strip. Continue to fold and lay strips crosswise until top is covered in lattice pattern. Trim overhanging strips. Moisten edges with water; pinch to seal. Crimp as desired. Use trimmings to make leaves. Place several leaves on top of lattice.

The combination of dried and fresh fruits in this tart creates a burst of flavor. Although directions are long, its preparation time is cut with the help of the food processor.

Preparation time: 45 minutes
Chilling time: 45 minutes
Cooking time: 20 minutes
Yield: 10 to 12 servings

CRUST

$1/2$ cup (1 stick) plus 2 tablespoons unsalted butter, cold

1 large egg

1 large egg yolk

$1/2$ cup confectioners' sugar

1 tablespoon whipping cream or milk

$1 2/3$ cups all-purpose flour

FILLING

8 dried apricot halves

5 tablespoons granulated sugar

2 large egg yolks

3 tablespoons all-purpose flour

$1 1/2$ teaspoons orange-flavored liqueur or vanilla extract

$2/3$ cup whole milk, scalded

$1/2$ cup whipping cream, whipped

FRUIT TOPPING

6 to 8 fresh apricots

8 small fresh strawberries

$1/3$ cup apricot preserves

1. For the crust, cut butter into bits. Combine in a food processor with egg, egg yolk, confectioners' sugar and cream; pulse on and off to combine. Remove the cover and add the flour. Process just until dough clumps together. Transfer to a large plastic food bag and press into a ball then flatten into a disk. Refrigerate 30 minutes.

2. Heat oven to 400 degrees. Roll crust on a floured board to a circle about $1/8$-inch thick. Transfer to a 10-inch tart pan with a removable bottom. Press into bottom and up sides. Trim excess dough. Refrigerate 15 minutes. Pierce dough in several places with a fork. Bake until golden, 18 to 20 minutes. Remove sides of pan and let crust cool on a wire rack.

3. For the filling, combine dried apricots and granulated sugar in a food processor or blender. Process until apricots are very fine. Add egg yolks and mix well; stir in flour and liqueur. Add scalded milk and mix well.

4. Transfer to a small, heavy saucepan. Cook over medium heat, stirring constantly, until mixture is very thick, 4 to 5 minutes. Transfer to a small bowl and whisk until smooth. Refrigerate until thoroughly chilled. Fold in whipped cream.

5. To assemble, spread filling evenly over crust. Cut apricots in half lengthwise and remove the pits. Cut into thin slices. Hull berries and cut lengthwise into thin slices. Arrange a circle of apricots around outer edge of tart; place a circle of strawberries inside the apricots and a circle of apricots in the center.

6. Melt preserves and push through a fine wire mesh strainer into a small dish. Carefully brush over fruit and top rim of crust. Refrigerate until serving time.

BASICS

BUTTER PASTRY

This rich pastry recipe is from Abby Mandel, who offers a tip for making your own convenient pie shells to freeze. She suggests making them in the food processor in consecutive batches. Then, after placing the dough in a large plastic bag, flatten it into a disc, then roll it, through the bag, to a circle about 8 inches in diameter. It freezes quickly and neatly this way and, when it is time to use, half of the rolling is already done.

Preparation time: 15 minutes
Chilling time: Several hours or more
Baking time: 20 to 24 minutes
Yield: One 9-inch single-crust pastry

$\frac{1}{2}$ **cup (1 stick) unsalted butter, well chilled**

$\frac{1}{4}$ **cup ice water**

$\frac{3}{4}$ **teaspoon salt**

$\frac{1}{2}$ **teaspoon sugar**

1 cup unbleached all-purpose flour

1. Cut the butter into tablespoon-size pieces. Put in a food processor and chop by pulsing the machine on and off about six times. Add the water, salt and sugar and process until the ingredients are mixed, about 5 seconds. The mixture should be in small pieces.

2. Add the flour and process just until the ingredients begin to clump together; do not continue to process until a ball forms or begins to form.

3. Transfer to a large plastic bag. Working through the bag, press the dough into a ball, then flatten into a disk, about 8 inches wide.

4. If you are using the dough right away, it must be chilled enough to firm it before rolling. Refrigerate or freeze just until it is firm but not hard. It also can be refrigerated up to two days or frozen; before using, let stand at room temperature until it can be rolled without splitting.

5. Fifteen minutes before baking, place the rack in the center of the oven and heat the oven to 425 degrees. Have a 9-inch pie plate ready.

6. Roll the dough on a floured board to a circle about $\frac{1}{8}$ to $\frac{1}{16}$ inch thick. Lift the dough several times and brush the board with flour to keep the dough from sticking. Lightly fold the dough in half, then in

quarters. Lift to the pie plate or tart pan and position it with the point in the center. Unfold and ease it into the bottom and sides of the pan. Do not stretch the dough. Trim the excess, leaving about $\frac{3}{4}$ inch of dough beyond the upper edge of the pan. Fold the overlap under so there is a double thickness of dough around the sides. Crimp the edge to make a border. Prick the dough so steam can escape.

7. Refrigerate or freeze until firm. Line the pastry with aluminum foil, and fill the foil with dried beans or rice to weight the pastry. Place on a baking sheet for easier handling.

8. Bake 10 minutes. Remove the foil with the beans. Bake the pastry until it is lightly colored, 10 to 14 minutes longer. Cool before filling.

BASIC PIE CRUST

This pie crust recipe is the Tribune test kitchen's favorite. The butter adds flavor and the shortening makes a tender crust.

Preparation time: 10 minutes
Chilling time: 30 minutes
Yield: 1 double crust for 9-inch pie

2 cups all-purpose flour

$^1/_2$ teaspoon salt

$^2/_3$ cup vegetable shortening or lard, cold

2 tablespoons unsalted butter, cold

5 to 6 tablespoons ice water

1. Mix flour and salt in large bowl. With pastry blender or two table knives, cut in shortening and butter until mixture resembles coarse crumbs. With fork, stir in just enough water so that mixture gathers easily into ball. With hands, shape into ball. Cover in plastic wrap. Refrigerate 30 minutes.

2. Divide dough in half. Roll and fit into pan as directed by recipe. Fill and bake according to recipe instructions.

RASPBERRY SAUCE

Raspberry sauce can enhance cheesecake, ice cream or fresh fruit. Raspberry liqueur adds a special flavor.

Preparation time: 5 minutes
Yield: 2 cups

2 packages (10 ounces each) frozen raspberries in light syrup, thawed

$^1/_3$ to $^1/_2$ cup confectioners' sugar

1 tablespoon raspberry-flavored liqueur

1. Puree the berries with the syrup and $^1/_3$ cup sugar in a food processor, letting the processor run about 2 minutes.

2. Pour sauce through a sieve to remove the seeds; stir in the liqueur and additional sugar as desired. Sauce can be made in advance and refrigerated for up to 3 days or frozen up to 2 months.

CHOCOLATE SAUCE

Rich and satiny, this sauce keeps for several days and can be served warm or at room temperature.

Preparation time: 15 minutes
Cooling time: 30 minutes
Yield: 2 cups

4 ounces unsweetened chocolate, chopped

1 cup granulated sugar

1 tablespoon unsalted butter

1 cup whipping cream

1 tablespoon brandy

1 teaspoon vanilla

1. Melt chocolate in top of a double boiler over warm water.

2. Combine melted chocolate, sugar, butter and half of the cream in a medium saucepan. Cook and stir over medium heat until smooth. Add remaining cream and stir to blend well.

3. Continue to cook mixture over medium heat, stirring constantly until sauce thickens slightly, about 5 minutes. Do not let it boil or scorch.

4. Remove from heat and allow to cool 30 minutes. Add brandy and vanilla; stir to blend well. Continue to cool to room temperature before using.

STRAWBERRY SAUCE

Perfect for topping ice cream, poundcake or puddings, this versatile sauce also can be made with a pint of fresh strawberries when in season.

Preparation time: 5 minutes
Yield: 2 cups

1 bag (1 pound) frozen strawberries, thawed

¼ to ½ cup water

4 to 5 teaspoons confectioners' sugar

1. Put the thawed strawberries in a food processor or blender. Process until smooth, about 1 minute. Add ¼ cup of water and 4 teaspoons of sugar. Process to mix. Check for consistency and taste. Add more water and sugar if needed.

2. Pour sauce through a sieve to remove seeds if desired. Refrigerate for up to one week or freeze for up to 2 months.

CREME FRAICHE

Creme fraiche hails from France, where fine cooks always have a bowl or jar of the tangy cream ripening on a kitchen shelf or counter. It is delicious spooned over fruit desserts, cakes or puddings.

1 cup whipping cream, not ultrapasteurized

2 tablespoons sour cream or buttermilk

1. Heat whipping cream in a small saucepan to 85 to 90 degrees. Remove from heat and whisk in 2 tablespoons sour cream or buttermilk.

2. Let stand in a warm place, covered loosely, until slightly thickened, about 8 to 12 hours. Stir well and refrigerate at least 8 hours before using. Creme fraiche also can be whipped.

BROWN SUGAR CARAMEL SAUCE

Try this sauce over bread pudding or apple pie slices.

Preparation time:
5 minutes
Cooking time: 5 minutes
Yield: 2 cups

---

1 cup (1 stick) unsalted butter

1 pound light brown sugar

¾ cup whipping cream

2 teaspoons bourbon

1 teaspoon vanilla extract

1. Melt butter in medium saucepan. Add brown sugar and cream, stirring constantly until smooth. Cook over medium heat until no longer grainy, 4 to 5 minutes.

2. Remove from heat and add bourbon and vanilla. Serve hot.

VANILLA SUGAR

Vanilla sugar is available at specialty markets. To make your own, slice a vanilla bean lengthwise in half and bury it in a container of granulated sugar. Cover container. Let stand for at least two days, shaking container occasionally.

Vanilla sugar is delicious in iced coffee and sprinkled over cut fruit or as a sweetener for plain yogurt or whipped cream.